Pen

Sujata Jha

/ BookLeaf
Publishing
India | USA | UK

Penumbra © 2024 Sujata Jha

All rights reserved.

Sujata Jha asserts the moral right to be
identified as the author of this work.

Presentation by *BookLeaf Publishing*

Web: www.bookleafpub.com

E-mail: info@bookleafpub.com

ISBN: 9789360946265

First edition 2024

To (Late)Prof. Kalpana Jha who left for her heavenly abode on 7th Oct 2023, a woman with a graceful and a strong personality. All that her inner child couldn't express I hope to express some of those thoughts through my writing.

ACKNOWLEDGEMENT

To the universe who has worked with me to make my writing dream a reality.

To my husband, Major G Rajasekhar, a reasonable human who means something to me.

To Anil Kumar a hopeful father, Abhimanyu Jha (author of *A Dilli Mumbai Love Story*) a brother with a beautiful mind, Revathi and Laya my two creative offsprings, and Snowwhite my beautiful GS, who have given me millions of reasons to write.

To Leeann McGuinness, my one true friend who helped me overcome extreme sadness, gave me hope and courage and last but not the least, Miss Emily D, who has always been my inspiration and whose record of the number of poems I aim to reach.

INDEX

Green Wilting Tree

How tall are you
How short am I,
How strong are you
How frail am I

The path you take
The path I make,
How brave are you
How naive am I

The crooked you
The wicked me,
How flexible are you
How stubborn am I

You tether and wither
I gather and prosper,
You seal and heal
I kill the feel

Yet I am the real deal.

A Quiet Night of Fright

Out there in the dark,

In the middle of the night
No stars, simply flickering lights
Motorbike rowdies swerve
Bulldoze Me into fright,

An Aimless Walk,

Howling winds, tired limbs
Just a feeling of lame and shame
Call up foes or friends
Oh No! Might just wait for light,

At Dawn,

Someone hears me shout
Calls me out
It's Life it says
Don't be impulsive with fate,

Wisdom will return,

See the morn near
Quiet my dear
Hope no one sees your tear
You are the one with fear,

Oh! Just be,

Without expectations
Accept limitations
Blame no one you clown
You bring this devastation,

On Yourself,

Believe in no one I pray
Not even He
Can turn the clock
Hurt is designed to mock,

Forever ties end in sighs
Fight your fears,
Go bravely through this night
To see your own halo light.

The Beggar

He looked like us
He was asking for sunny
My father didn't like the fuss,
And neither did granny

I asked him to work for us
My mother laughed funny
The angst on the man's face,
Made my sister snatch my penny

She called him away from us
Wiped his nose runny
Ah! A moment of kindness,
More valuable than the money

He looked amused by us
Ah! Kindness and penny
Together was a miss on most days,
A grin broke out like pure honey.

Hounded Grounded Heart

Dance Dance Dance away
A heartbreak
All shook up
Now or never
Shy away, just fly away

Sing Sing Sing away
A heartbreak
Let's be clever
Now or never
You ain't close, get far away

Always on your mind
Can you do the grind

Break the bond
Now or Never
Lie anyway, stray miles away

Pray Pray Pray away
Oh! grief stay away
Send me a ray
Now or never

A little bit of sunshine and hay.

Summer Holidays

Sleps are Stippery
Don't run jittery,

Mommy's chant
Made the little one rant,

Goblin games
All up in flames,

Missing shoes
Brought her blues,

A trip to the park
Made her a lark,

Ringing bells
Ice Cream melts,

Summer dreams
True it seems.

The Cook's Timeless Love

The Cook's cookbook has a say
He goes through it every day
Creates recipes old and new
Adds a pinch of his gay,

Platters of garlic and shrimp
Potatoes, even aubergines limp
He turns into a delight
Ecstasy is just at the brink,

I am the new incredible
I have heard he is able
It's not perfection I seek
Just a seat at his table,

Bosses me luck
As he tosses me in the duck

Succulents me wet
Roasts me up till the neck,

The murmur gathers momentum,

Not boredom but excitement shakes with a hum
hum,

The more and few relish the new yum yum,

Recipe straight out of his book
He calls it Timeless Love.

The Cat, Rat, Bat and a Hat

There was a cat named That
There was a rat named This
There was a bat named Those
There was a hat named These,
That wanted This
This wanted Those
Those wanted These
To hide the ugly toes,
One day These
Found her muse
Took off with a rouge
Hair girl called Tease,
Those got sad
This went mad
That felt bad
These didn't mind a tad,
The next morning woes

Tease strutted with a rose
Next to This That those
Was, These with a pose,
Tease painted nails of Those
Cheese was bartered to This
Milk for the meowy soul That
They finally said adieu to These.

Not before Not after

Let's meet and greet
To remember the old guy tonight
Let's put on our true faces,

Remember those colors full dazes,

Come out childhood
And adolescence traces
Don't let them feel alone
In days of sickness
Creepy is loneliness,

One day it will be your turn friends
Do away with your excuses
Not before, Not after

A man sick must be visited
To remind him of his strength in tons
Only by loved ones.

I shall be happy when I am Queen

Volume up, Volume down
That's all I do dawn to dawn
Loss of control, mind torn
That's how I live in this town

No guillotine, No Rasputin
Cleaning windows with a grin
Just ordinaries downtown
That's how I live in this town

Something, to be stepped on
Loud plays the background
One and many tradition bound
That's how I live in this town

I gave blood, I shed blood
Want no more a life common
I will be happy when I am Queen
That's how I will live the rest of the dream.

Gateway to Hell

School bell rings,
Doors open with a bang
Heart further sinks
Shoes nearly drag
Disturbed self, No inner harmony
On most wasteful days long
Tosses about in agony
Subjects Study stinks,
Food for thoughts cold
Tales transport horrors
Of another world old
Incapable some,
Feed on confidence kills
Friends or Foes, No one knows
Weird morals upheld,

New ideas shelved
Old ideas again read
Guise of new beginnings
Long bills for future frills,
Breaking backs
Wreak havoc,
On many sinking ships,
Ones who never question these horrors,
Get to cross,
The gates of hell
Piggybacks
On destiny of other souls.

Daughter

A new bud
Proud of her luck
Sways with an angel's grace
Plays with my heart
Face to face

Petal whispers an art
Tinkling laughter a dart
Fragrance fragile
Plays its part

Through my window's lace
With excitement she peeps
A sudden gaze
A look at my face

And she suddenly weeps
It gives me the creeps
A quick question deep
What's wrong my sweets

A race on her own pace
Win against time, just like me
Yet fall from grace
Reflects my end, hopefully

Not hers,

A pat makes her bright
We get through the night.

Caregiver

She parts my hair two ways
Dripping oil, grip her hands
Lifting the weight off my shoulders,
Head lets go of the sieving sands,
Limp go my senses
Relaxation seeps
Through my soul and hers too
As my pain she heals.

The Wooing

Backwaters in my mind
Path full of butterflies of all kind
To escape the grind
A Lady goes to Sea

Frilly frock and umbrella I find
Shoes the colour of Orange rind
To dress my heroine of a kind

Following her footsteps behind
Her lover timid, shy struggles with a pint
Poor Pitiless draws a line

Wishes she prefers him her dine
Courage shall come in time
To break traditional wooing rhyme
To become a truly blind

Takes a lot of Spirit.

An Unhealthy encounter

Found myself in front of the hospital
One day,

Billing counters were all full
To my dismay,

Waited with bundles of files
Swatting flies for my play,

The receptionist in black overhaul
Yamaraj in disguise that day,

I chuckled with delight
Sent some folded bills his way,

Greedily he smiled
Talked me to death as I paid,

I humbly asked for which sins
Of Past Present Future that lay,

Thorns or Roses, He said
Guess your fate, Oh Yes! You may,

Wait and Eternity
Is all coming this way,
Merry Go Round
On display,

No choice of None
Either this or that way!!

Braindead

Indistinct chatter around me
They all want to kill me

Dick and Jane
Cooing gasping grasping
Uh-huh Uh-huh
Grunting Ah Hm Huh!
Babbling chuckling sighing
Heh Heh Heh!

Am I dreaming
Got up screaming panting
They do want to kill me

Guess what
I can't be killed
I just ain't gonna die
Cause no one is listening
Hi-Yah Hi-Yah
I am dead in my head
Though my body is in bed
Funny Funny Funny
Spot I am in
Brain dead they say
Yet everything going in

Jump Jump Jump
Up and down
Come on kill me
I won't frown
I need to be killed
Look Look See now
I don't want you to kill
Just find me a way up the hill
It's time for me to go
To meet Jack and Jill.

Only if I was God,
I would know what to do

But,

Does God also know,
Or does he have a clue

How,

To heal people,
Bodies and minds too

Or,

Is he as clueless,
As me and you
And,

Are we just puppets,
Mindless creations to woo

With,

False tales of valour,
Limited to external battle woes

For,

Inner demons remain,
Waiting for solace to fly unto you.

A Fishy treat

Parrot fish wants more pancakes
With her fins flaying and dagger dart,

Eyes give me looks
That says, just a tiny part,

Hiding under the tortoise, plays
Trick or Treat
Flawless sharp patient wait
Games of a different Art,

Me clueless of her plans
Sits admiring while she charts
The course of cut to chase,

Bite your Bits
Give me mine, She quietly says

And departs,

My hand moves at most tops
Makes the drops right,

She comes along hops
Watch her feat
She makes a kill,
Feel the joys
My pet toys
With me and my heartbeats.

Rehabilitation

The car parked below
Someone came with a wheelchair in tow,

The patient looked for one that was low
He was not at all tiny in
Top and toe,

They found one and tucked him
Nice and tight as per his whim,

Loose ends made him grim
He was not at all slim,

They pulled him to the lift
Just a shift,
From low to up
yet deft,

Politely they left,

The doctor met the guy
Humourous soul not the usual dry,
This man remained a little shy
To even see the sky,

Was this such a big task
Like Do or die
I sigh,

The gentleman could not fly
Even in his mind
Will he do the grind,

Or

Will it be another bye
I hope not,

I will try just once more.

A Party for Married People

Just the two of us,
Keep changing our colours,

Warm to cool
Quiet to noisy
A home here,

A home there
Lonely with friends
Lonely without

Love only can fill the void,
See it seep through bad
These days

Clearly talks are not on the table,
Yet what seems doable

Is Party hard in duet,
Why not in Phuket

Dig deep and bury respect,
Manners laid out in baskets
Thrown out to sea

Scream your lungs,
Kick the sands
Of times desperate

Fall from grace,
Lash out the waves

Of graves and riches,
Moonlight and beaches
Calm yourself preaches

Rejuvenate the senses,
Go back to the crutches
Pick up the pieces

And Your self.

Lord of Immersions

O Lordship!
You finally arrived,
Did you take a tour of the world,
Or was it again around your parents My Lord,
Ah! In that case you must have missed the
devastation,
At that rate,
Would you really want to celebrate,
You might just create a bigger mess
I berate,
Those big mounds of boon,
Which are going to be dunked sometime soon,
Somewhere in a beautiful lake or river,
The same holy water, My giver

I do wish to save my liver,
Pomp and show of few days I can't fathom,
I am sure you live in every atom,
Just help us do our deed,
Bless us all,
And from our grace Pray not fall,
I earnestly plead!

Night always talks

Ringing the blood
Brain meets ears,
Deafening footsteps
I always hear,

Arrgh! My bedstand head
Creaks and cracks,
Oh! The shoes of leaves
Up my window peeps and creeps,
Makes my night haunted feats
Terrible Tricks or Treats,

My heart misses many beats,

Dawn is near it's time for bed
Snowflakes begin to fall on the doorstep,

White ghost does rhythmic walks
Can't sleep a wink
Night always talks.

I know why Siddhartha ran away

I know why Siddhartha ran away
Most of us have also thought that way
But he did the deed, a terrible need
To wash the grief of the world at play,

There was no place to stay
No single hope of ray
Looming large was a tree with roots deep
Yet, a very gentle sway,

Deep in thought he was that day
Time passed, he had nothing to say
One day, hunger overtook and lead
Him to seek alms as he had gone astray,

People were overjoyed they say
To meet little needs in a strange way
Kind deeds never went unpaid
It helped to think that they may,

Someday be moulded in Siddhartha's clay
Would be easy to just role play
With scripts defined and story intertwined
It would be just another way,
To run away
Not stay
Chaos, Mayhem a heavy cost to pay
By the near and dear in the name of duty
If I may say!!

Metamorphosis

Food water air
Just basic needs now,
Need to look for her
Run circles my eyebrows,
Put chaos into order
The only question how,
Journey to find the other
Picture yourself in tow,
Lucky will be you
To take that bow,
And turn into a Man
Seek same desperate fervour
Hunger to never lie low,
She will complete you for sure
More than anything else I know,

Having found the only cure
Time will reveal the truth,
Can you see the new colour
Turn bright red from dirty yellow,
Do your best a big favour
Take that vow,
Your transition pure
You must allow,
Miniature to Endure
Somehow
Become Mature.

Utility of Shadow

It peeped into my life
Enamoured by my generosity,
It decided to end its old rife
It wanted love, fame and prosperity,
Said It would always be on my side
Now that I have given it a new life,
Struggles uphill brought downside
Games began with Jekyll and Hyde,
It couldn't do it straight to my face
It couldn't splash fun
It couldn't kill my vibe
It couldn't hide
It couldn't die
It couldn't lie,

It began to take jibes
At shared insides
Spat venom and cried,

Curses far and wide
My shadow,
It was mid-day soon,
It left.

A Pilgrim

Meet my eyes O lover
Come a little bit to the front
Let's shake hands

Tell me your name
Let's embrace,

If you still don't love me
I will leave in grace
To a foreign land,

A beautiful journey awaits
And all it takes is
A little bit of you
And a little bit of me
And a little bit of time,

If you're sad
If you are in doubt
Scream out loud
Ask me to go
Don't be in pain,

I will know you don't love me
I will leave in grace
To a foreign land.

Are you sure we are dishonest

Are you sure,
We are dishonest, I say Yay!
Let us ask just three people
Who we meet on our way
If you are , all of mine isn't yours
Forever from this day
If not, all of yours is mine
You will have no say,
First one with a loincloth,
Lied for sure
He preached in a temple
Where God was made of stone
Took their money from them
Asked them their sin to atone,

Second man in a suit
He built people's homes
Broke the tombs
Of past lives pure
An act of lure
Tread carefully for doom,
Third one is me
Making a fool of you
Just like a politician
Whom we choose
False promises
A big black boon,
Ditch honesty
Not A difficult find

In

Day to day
Daily grind,

In

Hard Times,
People simply don't mind

A little bit of dishonesty.

No pain No gain

Jungle Jungle
You are spotted,
I have come to mingle
Can see you, in pain
Black and brown dotted,
Who is out to gain
Make some noise
O tender hearted,
For your own cause
To shake your ground

Dangerous plans concocted,
Flora, Fauna most eat dead
Rake the earth

Bring out emotions unbottled,
Save your hearth
Your home and all our hearts rotted.

My favourite people are turning strangers

Oh! How much I love,
All the seeds I have sown
To avoid any unknown
How much I love my own,

My favourite people
The unknown scares
Broken heart dares
Scraped knee flares,
Not my destiny
I seek No agony,
But My favourite people

Ah! Who are you,
How you know me better

You even sent a letter
Your Whispering words,
Make me tremor
Oh! My favourite people
His open heart
Immersed in the page
Tears embedded with rage,
Freed my heart from its cage

Ah! My favourite people
Don't become strangers
I fell in love with another,
Let me just savour
The splendour of the shelter of my fender.

Ambition is an energy drain

Did you have a nightmare,
Or
Did fear overtake you,
Or
Just sleeping alone
overwhelms you,
Or
The strangers around creep you
Or
When you are lost, horror meets you,
What is it about ambitious uncertainty,
That leaves you with darkness,
Feels like drowning in a pool of unknown
outcomes,
Are you really going to live in fear then,

For all the next moments of your life
Are nothing but many uncertain moments,
Forever running after the imaginary.

Thumb on a bruise

I am on a beautiful cruise,
Overcast skies
Shrieking gulls,
Dolphins display
Diving skills,
Bouncy Waves
Surfers Paradise,
Sunny eggs
Chocolate pies,
Behind Unknown desires
On unknown roads,
Heart crosses boundaries

A dream destination
It sees and seeks,
I fall from the bed
Hurt on my head
A thumb on a bruise
Wakes me up from the dead.

People who cry

People who cry
While sharing a feeling,
There is always
The first step of denial,
The hidden reality
The second step of exasperation,
Brings better clarity
The third step of loathe
An expressive self pity
The fourth step of dare
No more care, just verity
Save the innocents
We need fidelity,
Save the expression

We need integrity,
Save the soul
Keep their solidarity,
Crying is not about weakness
It's about courage simply.

The Head with a crown

I,
Find Easy to be true
Crows pickling on crabs amusing too
Sunset yellow rejuvenating sky blue
God's country just liberates a few,
I,
Find brokered harmony a good tool
Exist in peace smart fool
Imposing issues deal cool
Forbidden talents learnt soon,
I,
Find uncertainty a regular bloom
Enduring pain a big boon
Resolve conflicts like shifting dune
Live life not being crooned

I,
Find new sets of eyes
Looking out for a brighter sky
Bending down laces tie
Ready to get set go and die,

Sharing the vibe of the head with a crown

Don't follow blindly, you may drown.

'Ode to the City of Joy' - Kid collect

City of Joy,
From up above
Just a toy,
I dip into the clouds
Must be a coy,
Cruising below left and right
At thirty-five thousand feet, Oh boy!
Food for thought
Sunlit Windows
Hazy Sky
Junglee Sandwiches Masala chai,
I spot Belur
Amidst the sky,
And then duck right down

In the Hooghly on the sly,
In out up and down
My mind ducks and dives,
Watches boats and sails
Sell a lie,
Rejuvenates
Roams tirelessly,
Shrunken mind exterminates

Survives the fall, Just doesn't die!

No matter what a woman does

No matter what a woman does
It's never enough,
A corner room and a broom,
Too high too tall
Judgement swoons
On our tiny crowns,
Bowed heads making beds
And garden tends
Yet Time shreds,
Whatever little we make
Of ourselves,
What a dread,

Unforgiving rules
Compromises too soon,
Different Standards to the moon
And back bucking the trend
The only ones that can stand
Straight is the Buckingham bend,
Bonding on silly virtuosity
And a whole lot of pretend,
An important question to fend
Is what is truly noble to lend
Your ears to,
My dear friend,

To Unlimited theatrics of acclaimed people with
class mobility
Or to a house guest's inspiring tales of the
common nobility.

Selfless a myth - Pandemic Time

Who is wrong, Who is right
It's a question, a daily fight
Someone says it's perspectives
Everyone with different narratives,
Of obligations in hindsight
Towards each other's needs and plights,
Fulfilling random necessities
And survival even of their besties,
Turn into scary fights
Tales of Doubts and breaking treaties,
Are regularly believed stories
Relatives and friends tell eeriest,

Contribute with all their might
In Saving pleasures and not the Kite,
That is the heart trying escapes
From the clutches of the righteous knights,
Not really so much in their actions
Unwise suffocating parasites,
Is what they truly believe are us
Even then they sweetly fuss,
They are the worst lot
Ugly bickering pots,
Wish to lay them to rest
Was never so much felt!

Blain and Pouring

Japanese cheesecake
Blain and Pouring
Pineapple flavoured
Anniversary roaring,
In our face
Twenty Scoring
Chocolate Dark
Nights Soaring,
Birthday Boy
Seems boring
Get a spark
To keep him going,
Search the cellar
Under the staircase creaking
Bottles Bottoms up
Cheer goes dancing and singing.

Feel Good

Feel Good of
The rustic eyes
By faith
Were hurt,
Shy and yet tries
To grasp
Their doubts,
The battered remains
Brings mistrust,
Less gratitude
Has become their guide,
Reality bites, an acquired taste
Let's not believe in it,

Imagination is better
Hope is going to get a surprise,
When They call her back to Life.

Imposter

As I shifted from house to house,
Someone was shifting shapes
Physically elegant and mentally jubilant
I meet a different personality,
I just become aware of changes
Unseen yet, some temporary
Yet many permanent,
A daughter straight and my back bent.

Just Seal with a Kiss - Pandemic Moments

When you put a pen to seal someone's fate
Not everyone is Jack and Kate
Not everything is etched in the sands of time
One simply may just get an expiration date,

Why, Why, Why O Mate
One simply sighs
Heavy decision or light
For a dear one,
Even when on deathbed they lie,

How, How, How O Mate
To deal a rare occasional high
And more often the many lows
Morning, noon and at midnight,

More, More, and More
As Years pass galore
Only a few of us are
Anointed knights,

Sure, Sure, Sure
For once I am sure
We can't relive
The fright and the fight

No need for a warrior tonight
For now, Let's just seal it with a kiss
And say our goodbyes and goodnight.

No excuses

Do animals confess
May be they have animal perspectives
On how to make a better world,

Do they have identity issues
May be their imaginations
Can criticize the biased attacks,
Do they believe in reforms
May be they have camouflages
That see through political farces,
Do they want the processes
May be they only want automations
That reflect evolution's positive confirmations,
Is it not then about the foundations
May be if one really cares
That we exist together today matters
Never more.

Overweight

Burn, Burn, Burn
Isn't that the solution,
Lose weight stay healthy
Says the new generation
Cost, Cost, Cost
What Happens to Metabolism,

Work hard, play hard
Chants the Nation
Loss, Loss, Loss
Isn't there an energy drain,
Share and care
Only Boasts and all lame

Magic, Magic, Magic
There is none,

Show some constraint
When you simply eat my son.

Hidden pregnancy

I hide my bosom
I hide my bottom
I hide my hide
I hide my soul,
I hide my joy
I hide the toy
I hide the high
I hide the low,
I hide the year
I hide the tear
I hide the cry
I hide the shy,

When moon isn't bright
The dark is night
I begin a scream
Around my leg there is a stream,
I no more hide the hide
I no more hide the soul
I smile a satiety
I sing with gaiety.

Are you Whole or is there a Hole

Almost loved
Are you!
Almost courageous
Are you!
Almost truthful
Are you!
Almost successful
Are you!
Something about almost
A great deal of being short
Full of holes
A lot of different
From the whole.

Birthday Bites

Knock me off my feet
This birthday this year
May be the way you will say my name
Wish me not lame
Will make it all right,
I have never done what I was told
Today forty seven, but start to feel old
May be if I get some shining streaks
Eat some scrupulous steaks
Will make it all right,
Sitting on the threshold
Seeing time just disappear
May be if l roam around just holding hands
Clear drinks with handsome lads
Will make it all right,
Worry about everything and everyone
So much heavy, nothing light

May be if I worry about myself
Dance with singing elves
Will make it all right,
Blues, Greens and Browns
Frown upon me the clown
May be if I laugh with them
Not on them dame
Will make it all right,
Bake them in tons
Call them all
Cake Everyone
Spongy wholesome
May be this time it will taste right,
Much interesting left behind
Much scintillating up front
May be just breathe
Is what I need for tonight.

Hollow Horns

A King of a kingdom prosperous
A man kind and religious
Had remained childless
After many years of prayers
A son born brought happiness,
Yet a terrible secret was theirs that dawn
The Prince had horns
When he was born
The King was distraught and torn
While the Queen put out a mourn,
The royal barber shaved Prince's head
To secrecy he was sworn till death
He began to suffer from a stomach ache
Deep in it up till his neck
Could not shake off his dread,

Went to a tree
Shared his misery
Pain disappeared in a jiffy
Went about his drudgery
The tree was sworn to secrecy,
One day the tree fell down
A drum was made in town
For the drummer to play a sound
It sang out loud
The Prince has horns on his head,

The King went mad
The Queen turned sad
The barber was warned
Truth was told
A Pardon was sold.

Memories of Yesteryears

Moonlight and the swing
The birds sing sing
Thoughts linger
For a moment
And then bring,

Memories Memories
of yesteryears,

A simple flower ring
The church bell ding ding
Hearts wonder
To unite or not
In Spring,

Memories Memories
of yesteryears,

A veil so long
The clock ding dong
The casket shivers
Ground devours
Sweetheart on a whim,

Memories Memories
of yesteryears,

Joy and sorrow cling
A phone tring tring
A dull moment never
Life is clever
Fills up to the brim,

Memories Memories
of yesteryears.

Waiting for Downpour

Rain Rain
Wash away my pain
Break away the spell of dry
Remove each and every stain,
Take away everything vain
Give back my energy drain
Shimmering Showers
Always keep me sane!

'My little one' - Kid collect

When She was born
There was no sound at all
She lay quiet
Not as per norm,
Tightly fisted pink overall
Curly black ringlets as a crown
Peeped out the blue shawl
And then there was that frown,
That said,
Why the hell did you fellas wake me up 'n' all
And Now that I have woken
You guys better be ready for an overhaul!
Run up and down, Do a merry-go-round
On the count of three
Now, Go fetch me a ball.

Reality of Real estate

He wanted to sell a house
I wanted one without a mouse
How excited I was to own a pouch,
He said and smiled nice
Don't worry there will only be mice
And we shall trap them all with a slice,
Of perk control but then lie,
Kill them without a sigh
And they shall definitely die,
I wasn't too sure of the mice
And nor the man playing dice,
Who was plainly after the booze
and the hen garlicky slice
Dipped in mayonnaise, cash
And brimming entice,
Let there be light
Here is some advice,
A crystal clear deal of supply

And demand determines the buy
Yet Everything is at an unrealistic price
There is nothing real about haggling nice
Make sure to not pay a heavy lie,
For a piece of heaven only you define
Find just comfortable for a life nice
To kill the cacophony of my house and I.

Daughters' day

Daughters live in quarters
They belong nowhere
Yet can be seen everywhere,
Where reality strikes
Or someone the dust bites
However complicated the path
However much her own wrath
Yet an open mind she keeps,
Not peeves but paves
Ways out of conflicts
Always in control
even if it demands shifts,
And sacrifices of her own
Aspirations that she keeps
Hidden in her heart and weeps
Sometimes and hopes,
To see them fulfilled it seems

Isn't the destiny she seeks
Cause she unknowingly knows
What the other needs,
Knows not how
To turn her back,
Now that's a serious lack
So all I can wish for her is pure dumb luck.

With a little luck never

With a little luck never
Should I have to see wildfires
Should I have to meet flat tires
Should I have to stage parties
Should I have to do false charities
Should I have to eat junk fries
Should I have to diet for weight loss tries
Should I have to tell lies
Should I have to fake cries
Should I have to break relationships
Should I have to sink some ships
Should I have to buy gold stones
Should I have to hide and see them turn old
Should I have to comply
Should I have to kill flies

Should I have to be in deep mess
Should I have something bad to confess
Should I have to live a lie
Should I have to be afraid to die
With a little luck never
Should I have to live ever
Without You.

A cloud song

What if the clouds sing
What would they sing about
May be about thundering
Even about losing identity
Or just about
Floating high in the sky,
May be about silver skies
Shining stars losing light
Or just about
Pouring hard with all their might,
May be about end of dry
Glittering tears and hidden pain
Or just about
A lot of prosperity and gain,
May be about hither and thither
This or that

Or just about
Their own bits and pieces when the rain falls.

Flyover woes

There is a new flyover
This flyover makes me fly
Driving in the wind
Somehow makes me cry,
We got married here just last July,
There was a house
They broke it down
My partner took the money
Like a clown,

He is a rider very shy
Up and down we cry yet try
Faster, and then brakes we apply
With fear and excitement
His mouth goes dry,
It's so lovely he says he may die

Rules of engagement matter
He didn't comply,
Betrayal is hard to get by
Marriage is but do or die,
Hope I miss us
As we ride into the sky
We didn't get to say goodbye
We just got married last July.

Value Yourself

Can you respect my time
Of which I have little
When you promise a dime
Don't give a nickel
Endless wait increases fury
I Not playing a second fiddle
Unnecessary worry
Force me to become uncivil
I will take out the pistol
I will lay it down next to the sickle
I will put tea in the kettle
I will wait for the whistle
And You.

Hope Kills

To keep alive a tradition
Hook the one glad
Give care to take it all away
Make one forever sad
Bestow abandonment too,
When it gets tough a tad
Joke and laugh all the way
To hide the chaos and grief at bay,

Here there and nowhere

Nothing but despair and despite,

In this prison of eternity

No need of a rope
Just give hope
And kill one mercilessly.

I understand

There is nothing left to save
Once in your deep dark cave
About the good olden days,
How much ever the rave!
Come away
Hush the sway
Look from far,
Don't be at war, I pray
With yourselves
In the fight with elves
Take a stand, Not understand,
And see their disappointed selves.

At the Beach

If that's a cave
I am a slave,
The water is pink
The one I drink,
Not the waves
They are blue,
All this is true
If you are naive.

Kill Me Softly with a Life
Song

In life prejudices are fought alone
Sins of mine do atone
Calm the mind
Stop being a pawn,
In the name of love
Together fly the doves,

When deeds destined take priority above
Not even one is on your side
Saving their hides
Friends and Foe simply sigh

Leave you out to die.

A death of shame
For your lame
Thoughts and deeds
Of forever,

Go You! Play the game once again
Save your name
Lose the Love,
Don't kill your grace
Don't lose your face.

Face to Face

I have two faces
A straight face
One that knows the right
Puts on the necessary dress
Acts out necessary parts
Smiles and makes it all right,

My other scarface is sure of your lies
Barely told twisted truths
In Life and otherwise
And when I go places
You fall from my graces,

Every day the faces fight
Oh, yes! What a sick sight

With curled and fists tight
I fall asleep and dream
Of Father and Mother all night,

Nonetheless I keep a straight face,
Alas! Before, My scarface wakes
Let's do a shake
Mix merge bake
To produce a fake
Smile, just one take

Dear, Please don't wait
You aren't my soul mate.

Juno finds Gold

Brothers and Sisters
Went to the moon
Came back with a stone
And named it "Precious boon",

They got happy-go-lucky,
Youthful and divine
Ready to mould
They sang tales of the heist
Convinced of the told,

They played,
Up together Down together
Front together Back together

The stone rested in their bosom
As Life changed seasons,

When it was time to let go,
A Fight so cold
Sealed their souls
Fought more when they got old
Yours or mine whose is the stone,

I, the worthy one
Deviate from the told
My path must unfold
Way to merge all our spirits with
Fertility and prosperity in our fold,

Behold!
No cheats, No lies, No evil
No kill shall be sold
Brave stories only told
Shall keep us warm from cold,
Just be merry like the devil
Smile away the unknown perils,
Abandon the stone
Let bygones sing condone
Be ready to leave the known
Be ready to leave home.

'Perch' - Kid collect

The Kite sat on a big Gulmohar tree
For free,

The Seven Sisters closed up on a plea
To disagree,
The company was completely unexpected
Absolutely unnecessary,

Their Predator dark and dreary
Perched eerily,
The Danger imminent clearly
Definitely scary,

They planned immediately and agreed
To oust the stranger at three,

What they could together foresee
Forced the loner to flee,
The seven continued on their
Peaceful food hunting spree!!

Karma

The Almighty gave me all
But the Man, Machine and Man-made,
Karma took a toll on me and made me afraid
Just like the Spanish flu had most dead,

On things overall
I suffered a maul
With innumerable marks on my soul,
Heart now I desperately need
A complete overhaul
And not a future inevitable philosophy feed,
Or a good fortune call

I have had a new itinerary made
After I have seen many dead,
On a journey alone I tread
With absolutely much dread,
There is this
Just but once, I wish to delay,
And to simply lay
Out of habit silver plates
For the savouries to be spread
To share with my loved ones,

Someone holds my hand
And says don't be afraid,
These are tactics of delay
Keep moving on
Don't worry about the end

Wherever you tread,
Whatever you achieve,
Together we have always soared!

For all new beginnings
You yourself have always been the lead
Unknowingly My friend!

'Teacher Teacher Burning Bright' - Kid collect

One fine day I decided to teach
Ah! It was going to be the tiny tots,
I was going to be a terror
And teach them to fear
And only then would I teach
And that would be my strategy,
What happened next
Was completely unexpected,
Though it was just tiny tots
They felt far out of reach
They measured me up and down
And laughed as if I was a clown
Flustered I rode up and down

Angered by the rejection
In tears I did drown,
But When they saw me cry
They suddenly all hushed
Around my table they gathered
And tightly they hugged
Me one by one
I was surprised,
Times of distress
Had turned me
A foe to a friend
A small bench of young ones
Had brought the up righteous
Me right down to my knees.
They had taught me better lesson plans
I went back to the words someone wrote
That child is the father of the man.

Envy

Breakfast on my table
Cause I am able
They envy me a lot
These small pots

They live without the riches
All they have is tender care and kisses
Their best friend is the rose
But they envy me my toes
They have no house to live
All they have is fresh air to breathe
Their life full of dappled colours
Yet they envy me for my dull summer

They have no one to worry about
All they have is peace and quiet

Their life spent as tranquility givers
Yet they desire my selfish years.

Deathly Desires

These days
Violence can be of many forms
People have made their own norms
Divided in Justified and not dorms,

They try to rationalize the deathly desires
Are proud of the little known
With Not much support of their brain own
Are caught in lame acts of desire lone
Not knowing the harm sown
Leave bitter prints on the soul forlorn
Be scared of games of such kinds
They all seem to haunt minds

The doer and the one torn
Have been witness on both platforms
Have felt the heaviness on both accounts
You have the choice of escape or head-on
The trick might be just one,
Need to overcome limitation
Need quick and independent decision
Ask for forgiveness for misdeeds done
And accept a new morn
In hope of a new dawn.

'Bewitched by a fish' - Kid collect

I wished for a fish
In my dish,
To entice my taste buds
And for sure enrich and nourish,
Yet suddenly
Found myself in a deep abyss,
While thinking of dethroning the Miss
I was clueless and amiss,

Ah! I found her boneless
A deep crisis averted,
Am finally glad
And ready to dig,
The heavenly taste that forever has
Me bewitch.

A recipe not for disaster

Miss Cauliflower,
beautiful light green florets,
Found herself floating
In ghee and mustards,
Accompanied with asafoetida
Just a pinch maybe less,
Golden brown lightly fried
Mr. Potatoes pleased
with his accomplished state
Wished the lady, hello mate,
We have found comraderies
Yet I have also invited
Salt and Turmeric a little late
To make the flavour truly great,

Ah! I am obliged
But you forgot someone

Miss Cauliflower cried
My best friends, Onion Ginger
Garlic and Peppers Grinded
To a smooth paste
Without whom I can't be tried,

Oh! My lady, He sighed
And quickly apologized
To make up for his folly
He requested Mr. Tomato red
specially plucked and pureed
To make rich the final juices
Of the deliciously made
Potato Cauliflower Curry.

Coping Mechanism -
Pandemic Times

Things happened
The helper soul warned,
Lost in the Debacle
An adult surfaced,

The real enemy is Understand
Against feelings underplayed
Loss of identity
Finds one depressed,

One is warned
Slowly butchered
Signs of deteriorate
Insane and naked,

Party has ended
Monster has resurfaced
Smile and hate
Works better instead.

'Peachy promise' - Kid collect

There is a way to fearlessly fly
Move to the left
Move to the right
Go up shooting straight
And then gleefully glide,
How are you doing up there
Just hold toasty tight
Target in straight sight,
If you want to peacefully perch
Brake a slightly sight
And there you leisurely land,
Find new random reasons
To fly hopelessly high
Promise me that you will give it a tough try,

Every single daunting day
Trust yourself
And your new hopeful horizons

To give you a fair playful play.

Magical Reality

What if I had a cooking pot that cooked
delicious and economical,
What if I had a roll of silk that when stitched
never grew shorter and to wear was comfortable,
What if I had a bag of grains that never ended its
supply and fed inexhaustible,
That's all that will be required
For me to have a good life able,
Ah! The law of Survival paused
Failure of the infallible,

I so love fairy tales
and the world magically capable,
With snowflakes and castles
And pink and pastel sables,
In my world
The extraordinary will have

Nothing to worry,
Just a bit of sherry
Will bring dreams starry
And make them reach
Places magical in a jiffy,
Land them on an island of cherry
Blossoms that bloom once annually,
Only Beware!

If I get bit by reality
Now that's a source of worry
I will definitely be sad and sorry
Will find myself in the land of the troubled
And the waters deep dangerous and murky.
So a word of advice, to the me merry
Stay away from foolish and predatory
And look! I will be safe on my ferry.

Sunday Shopping Woes

Have you ever shopped
Things up to the top
Of a shopping cart till you drop
Oh dear! Stop,
Think if you need
All those in the load
Else you may topple the boat
And feel like a sacrificial goat,
On top it all there is sweltering heat
Standing, Oh You are dead beat
You can feel your brow has met
With drops of hot sweat,
Wait! The ordeal is not just over yet
You have just made it to the billing pet
The long roll is yet to print
And probably will stop your heart beat,

It has probably been three months net
Since this harrowing destiny I met
And I haven't learnt anything yet
My middle-class saving mindset
Finds me today again in the same love nest.

'Happy Halloween' - Kid collect

Happy Halloween!
Scarier the better,

Oh! Give me an ear dear
Oh! I do want the real one
If you keep up the chatter,

Be careless,
So that I can eat you thoughtless,

Quickly have your treat and disappear
Or I shall have you all for supper!

Milton Keynes UK
Ingram Content Group UK Ltd.
UKHW050213210724
445674UK00023BA/591

9 789360 946265